BODY OF CHRIST

We say that the Eucharist is the center of our faith. But what does It MEAN? How easily the words "Body of Christ" slip off our lips without making the slightest impression on our lives!

Here are splendid, modern reflections on the great reality of the Eucharistic Sacrament which is inseparably linked to the flesh and blood sacrifice of Calvary. The Body of Christ is not just a piece of bread — it is a piece of life. There is a presence of Christ in the tenement as well as in the tabernacle.

Fr. Larsen's books have sold more than half a million copies. Read this latest one and you will see why.

Some other books by Earnest Larsen:

Don't Just Stand There
For Men Only
The Gift of Power
Good Old Plastic Jesus
Hey, I Love You!
Liturgy Begins at Home
Not My Kid
Why Don't You Listen?
You Try Love, I'll Try Ajax
Will Religion Make Sense to Your Child?
Treat Me Easy

Are there ALBA BOOKS titles you want but cannot find in your local stores? Simply send name of book and retail price plus 30¢ to cover mailing and handling costs to: ALBA BOOKS, Canfield, Ohio, 44406.

Earnest Larsen, C.SS.R.

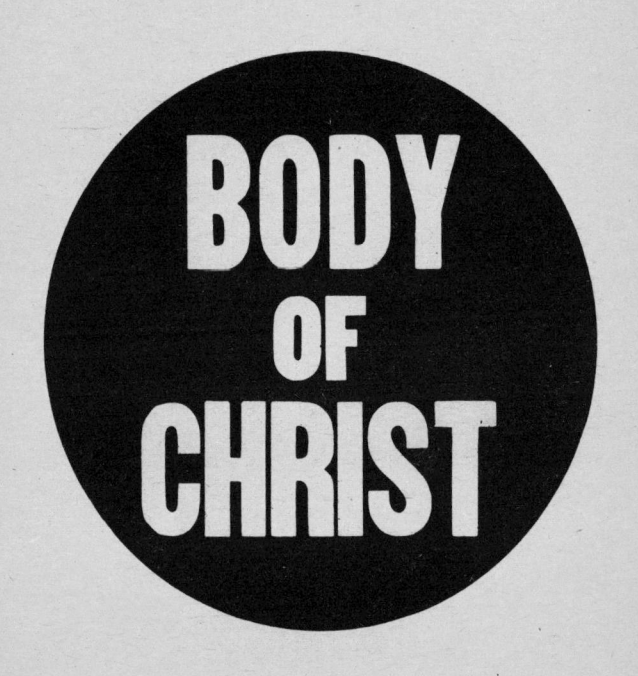

BODY OF CHRIST

ALBA BOOKS

NIHIL OBSTAT

Reverend James A. Clarke
Vice Chancellor
Censor

IMPRIMATUR

✝ James W. Malone

The Most Reverend James W. Malone
Bishop of Youngstown

March 12, 1976

Library of Congress Catalog Card Number: 76-6703

ISBN   0 — 8189 — 1134 — 4

© Copyright 1976 by Alba House Communications, Canfield, Ohio, 44406.

Printed in the United States of America

Artwork: Ron Wicklund

DEDICATION

To Michelle Welch
Ryan Fitzgibbon
and the fire
that burns
after sundown.

Table of Contents

1. *Eucharist as Courage / ix*

2. *Eucharist as Faith / 23*

3. *Eucharist as Healing / 47*

4. *Eucharist as Dialogue / 69*

5. *Eucharist as Gift / 95*

   Leave Christ / 113

*We create models
by which we interpret reality.*

*The problem is that these
become our prisons.
We create models
and they cage us in.*

*We all have a model
of the Eucharist.
But we lose much of the power
and meaning the Eucharist has,
because our minds don't carry
the meaning into areas of life
like dialogue, trust,
acceptance of God's love.*

1

EUCHARIST AS COURAGE

What does Eucharist mean?
Where does it happen?
How shall we know its power?
Those words making present that reality:
Body of Christ!
spoken to so many millions —
what do they mean?

BODY OF CHRIST

Tom was only 26 when
he died.
I knew him well despite the fact
he could neither walk nor talk.
Some people are gifts to others,
teachers of life's most important lessons.
Tom was like that.
His mind was a firefly, constantly alive,
darting, alert.
Although spastic he had good luck with a
word board,
(a large wooden square with the
alphabet and select phrases laid out.)
While using the board he would fiercely try to
still the tremors in his arm
and spell out with shaky finger the word
whose meaning
he desperately tried to share.

At times it didn't work; he would
pound his head, literally,
in frustration on the board.
The meaning was buried under a cloud of
non-comprehension and he
so desperately
wanted to be understood.
But when he did break through,
when meaning was communicated,
all the rainbows and sunshine in the world
poured from his face.
Uncontrolled joy as in Christ
being born again.

Tom and I struggled in this fashion
for an hour,
head pounding and all,
while he tried to communicate how much
he wanted a ride to the airport to greet
mutual friends returning from a long trip.
Tom knew!
He knew the date of arrival and
how much he loved them.
He knew the airline and probably the
name of the pilot.
I had no idea what he was getting at.
Frustrated terribly he would try one track with his
dull companion,
then another.
He dragged out pictures of the family returning,
made noises like a plane;
spelled the date of a month.
Pounded his head,
begged,
shook his head in amazement at my thickness.

But *then* it dawned!
An explosion of joy.
On the same track at last! We
even made plans to get presents for the family.

Over the years since Tom has died
I have often seen Christ in that
frustrated memory.
Head pounding on the board.
A most expressive person saying
over and over
you just don't get it!
Can't you see!

Meaning is the key.
Not just what a thing is but
what it means.
Tom and I both knew what a plane was — but
I couldn't break through his
meaning
of what it meant in bringing his beloved friends
home.
We missed on the meaning of things.
And, perhaps, so with Jesus.

At this moment in a hundred thousand places
a priest is holding bread in some form,
with more or less devotion, with
more or less spirituality he is saying,
"BODY OF CHRIST."
That is what it is.
We all know what Eucharist is —
Bread that is Christ.

This isn't the question.
That question is an intellectual consideration,
it can have countless books written on it,
a question lending itself more or less to a
solution.

The question of meaning is a
heart question.
It never ends.
Tom and I could, finally, communicate on
times of arrival and meeting the plane.
We could never communicate totally
on the meaning of his love.
In gifting one another we could walk that road
both growing in the Spirit of love,
but totally understand .... never.

And sometimes, personally,
I feel I can almost hear a groan slipping
from the consecrated bread —
so much like Tom,
You don't get it!
You just don't understand!
So depressingly often we expend fantastic energy
on what things ARE,
we attack, analyze, tear apart.
So seldom,
it often seems,
do we take the essential time to do nothing
and quietly sit before the temple of a Tom
or Eucharist, or love
reflecting on what a reality
means.
In silence secrets are told.

BODY OF CHRIST....

A body
that is an invitation.
From thousands of lips and hands and hearts,
Body of Christ....
into millions of other lips and hands and hearts,
into countless lives.

The invitation,
of what?
To what?
For what?

What does it mean?

What could Christ possibly be saying?

What power is there?

Far beneath the rather frigid surface of
just what Eucharist,
the Body,
IS —
what does it mean?

If we sit quietly before this temple
arising like a life-saving oasis in the heart
of our spirit's desert
what does it mean?

RIGHT QUESTIONS

It is an old saying that there are
no right answers to wrong questions.
Perhaps we often ask wrong questions
and so
find no satisfying right insights.

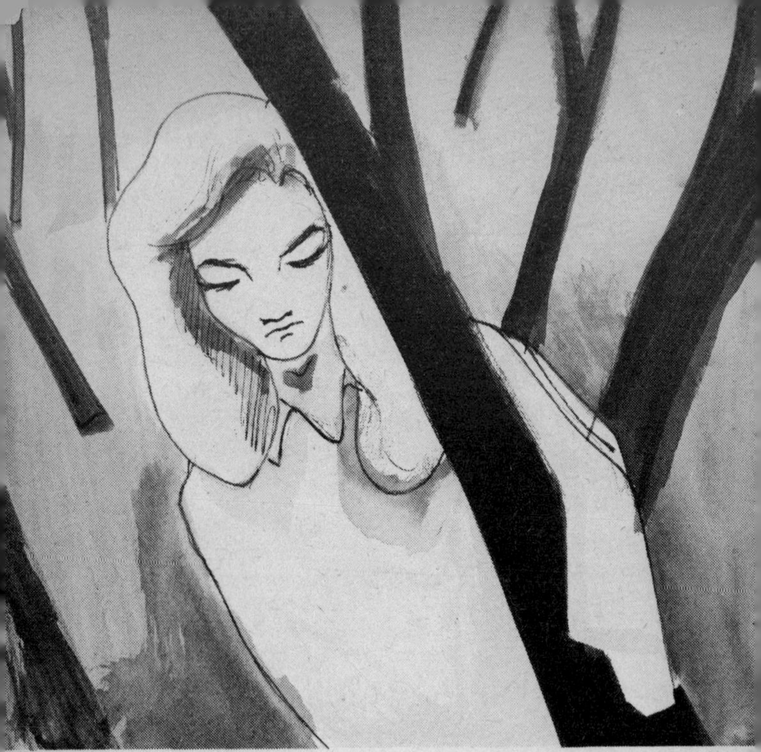

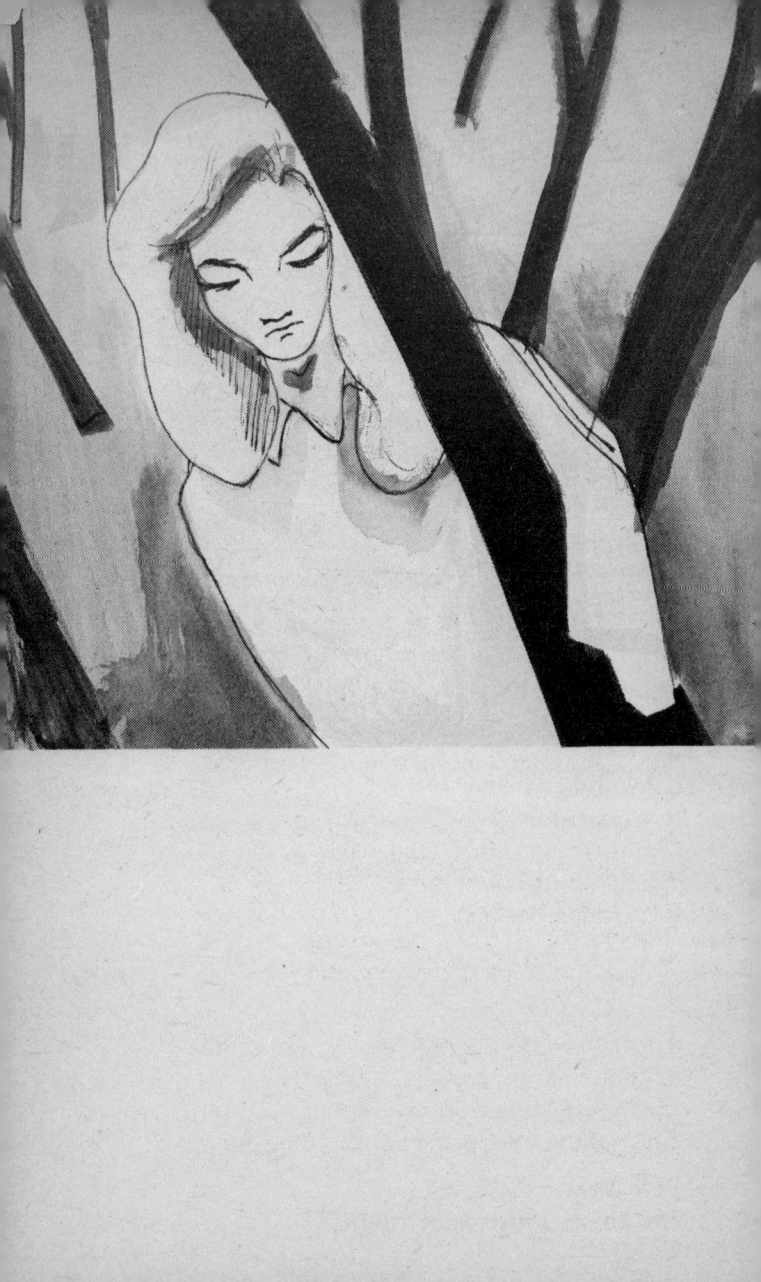

Possibly we have asked multiple wrong questions
concerning Eucharist,
as it now is held aloft in our mind's eye
in all those hands across this globe,
RIGHT NOW
as we quietly sit before this Temple of God
awaiting for the gift of his revelation —
and so have found "answers" rather than Christ.

Jan's face has been carved
by the cruel hand of a hard life.
She married out of high school
over 30 years ago.
The man was alcoholic even then.
She wasn't much less sick herself.
For 23 years they hacked and tore at
each other.
When it ended, 7 years ago, she sobered up.

Five of those years were good.
The last two, hell.
Two nights ago she got drunk.
It was the 26th of December.

Have you ever seen beaten, defeated,
wrinkled flesh basketed eyes weep?
Her tears flowed in and out of
the valleys of pain creasing her face.

"I'm tired" she said,
"So tired. I just want to die."

In Jan's mind if the whole world were a sign
it should be pointing to her saying,
"Here is a sinner,
a failure,
an object of hopeless, helpless humanity."
She believes that.
In her mind she is the ugliest person
on earth.
So we talked.

We talked about her loneliness,
her pain, her sense of failure.
At one point the rawest
of all shattered, stripped nerves was touched.
"It's love, isn't it, Jan.
It's love in all of us.
People aren't good or bad.
People are just hungry.
We all are.
So spiritually hungry to love and be loved.
If we find nothing to nourish our souls
we will eat anything.
To starve doesn't make you bad,
it just makes you vulnerable in your hunger.
It's love,
isn't it love, Jan?
Just wanting to love and be loved?"

Tears burst out.
Not merely from her eyes
but from the core of her being.

Tears wrung from streets most of us couldn't
imagine,
tears locked away from sounds and feelings
of such alienation and panicky fear
that only those close to the brink could know.
With eyes that have held the same look
since beings first became human,
eyes back to our ancestors huddled around an ice
age fire in the frozen history of our planet,
eyes of the first man who loved the first woman,
Jan looked up and said,
"Oh, yes, Father,
Oh, yes, how desperately I want to love
and be loved."

Hours later we split.
Before leaving I asked her,
"Jan, could we pray together?"
Then came the question,
the right question that can lead
to the right road.
pitiful as the question was,
from her valley of pain she said,
"Do you think He would mind?"

BODY OF CHRIST
What does Eucharist mean?
All those countless people looking up,
the host, priest held,
the words proclaimed,
Body of Christ —
But what do they mean?

Jesus in agony of wanting,
so desperately,
to crack through all the halting questions of
"Do you think He would mind."
Christ with aching head from banging it
on his talk board.
Christ in all his gentleness.

Jan and I held hands.
We prayed that we,
both of us,
would be more free to accept that
God has first of all loved us.

Casey asked,
"Is it a sin?"
A question Christians and perhaps
especially Catholics
seemed obsessed with.
In this situation it took on even more
incredible proportions.

Casey is only 16 and probably
alcoholic. If not that certainly
chemically dependent on something.
He won't admit it though despite
all the trouble he has been in,
most of his life,
constantly running from reality,
escaping into any alley he can find.
The latest one,
after three months of staying clean,
he had found a babysitting job.

He liked the people and the kids.
They were good for him.
But things started closing in,
he got scared,
depressed,
felt like running.
So he did —into booze and pills.
He ran instead of going to his job.
Left them, his friends, standing high and dry.
He doesn't know why.
Much of his life is out of his own
control.
What he said was,
"I want to go to an insane asylum.
Lots of times I act insane,
trying to get committed.
I have been kicked out of school lots of times
acting crazy.
I'm afraid one of these times I won't
be able to tell the difference though."

His questions about
"sin"
had nothing to do with any of his life.
His sister joined the
Jehovah Witnesses and was pressuring him to join.
He wanted to know if it is a sin to
go to a meeting.
He's not concerned about his
incipient insanity,
his chemical dependency,
his out of control life.
But sin gets him.

11

For Casey
Sin is what puts you in hell.
The ultimate rip off.
He has no questions about his own
joy or peace,
serenity or love —
but lots of questions about
sin and hell.

BODY OF CHRIST.

I met Casey after a noon Mass.
Of course he hadn't gone to communion.
No Eucharist.
That is for the good people,
those who deserve it.
Not him.
He is too ugly,
too crazy.
But what does Eucharist *mean?*
Where does it happen?
How shall we know its power?
Those words making present that reality:
Body of Christ!
spoken to so many millions —
but what do they mean?

Beccy is only 9 but
she knows —
or is beginning to know.
Like lots of beautiful little girls
she went to Santa at Christmas.
He asked her a routine question,
"Have you been a *good girl?*"

Shy as a butterfly she whispered,
"Yes."
Santa, then assured her of her wishes.

Later
at home she broke into tears.
She had lied.
The great bitter tears stung her father's heart
as they did her face.
"I'm not a good girl,
I am Bad.
I fight with my brother sometimes."
How soon we learn we are
bad.

How soon we shut the doors to our
all loving God.
Lots of people
Beccy.

One I know very much.
He is kind of a pack rat
who picks up little treasures all around
few seem to see.
Rocks, shells, twigs, ideas —
faces of transparent people,
one hand touching another,
tones of voice speaking wonder.

One of the bits of treasure this man
collected
was a large piece of fool's gold.
Beccy's tears had also stung him.

13

The immense tragedy of one so young and
beautiful,
learning so young and
deeply
"... that I am bad"
scalded his heart.
So he strung the iron pirate on a strip
of rawhide and wrote a poem about gold —
that all of us are seekers of gold.
We stand in the river of life with our pans
under the water
hoping, wanting very much
for some gold to wash up in our hands.
But people are the gold.
Love is the gold.

Beauty is the nugget above price.
He told the girl that she,
yes, SHE!
was gold in his pan.
The necklace was hers
IF
(there is always a price to be paid)
she would say each time she put it on that
she was gold in his pan.

BODY OF CHRIST!
The timid sun peeked out from behind
a cloud of gloom and self doubt.
Could she be gold?
Could someone love her?
Find her beautiful?
Could she really be sunlight in
someone's life?

Maybe so — after all
didn't she have a necklace and a large
golden stone
hanging around her neck.
It must mean something!
What does it mean?
What is the Body of Christ?

EUCHARIST AS COURAGE

Is it not possible often,
so tragically often,
to ask the wrong question from which
there can be no right road.

What is it?
What is Eucharist?
Can 'transubstantiation" really happen?
If so, what are the implications?
Who and how must
sacred be touched.

Not that any of these are
bad questions —
just perhaps for a time and people
disastrously perishing from
spiritual hunger
they aren't the most vital.

Perhaps for a Jan and Casey,
for a Beccy and Tom they aren't the
questions that make the most difference.

From that immense human scream
IS LOVE POSSIBLE?
IS IT POSSIBLE *FOR ME?*
other questions and other meanings
arise.

A hand to hold,
a heart to pray with is what Jan needed,
eyes to look compassionately into hers
without judging if she is good or bad
but only praying with her to
their common Father.
Let the debates rage in the halls of
academia —
she is neither for nor against them,
she really doesn't care.
It isn't the intellectual dispute
as to what it is
which she hungers for but
the reality of what it means!

Beccy needed to know,
to hear and see and touch
that she is sunshine,
gold in someone's pan.
On the wings of that love she will
experience
that BODY OF CHRIST
is for real.
That it IS power,
the power that casts out fear.

But it is no small thing to cast out fear.
The call is the challenge to courage.

It takes courage to love.
A subtle kind of course we often
dance around.

It is the paradoxical question of the
open door or wall.
Any sane person
obviously
would state that it is easier to walk through
an open door than a brick wall.
Given the choice we would always choose
the open door.
Only a fool would try to pass through a
brick wall.

That may well be
but it has yet to be proven that most people
would choose the open door.

An open door of relationship invites
trust, acceptance, vulnerability, —
all those ghost shrouded realities.
It declares,
"Hey, you don't have to go it alone.
I'll walk with you —
if you let me.
I'll touch your sorest wound —
if you let me.
I'll stand and face your ugliest part
with you —
if you will let me.
I will celebrate your depression and your
joy —
if you will let me.

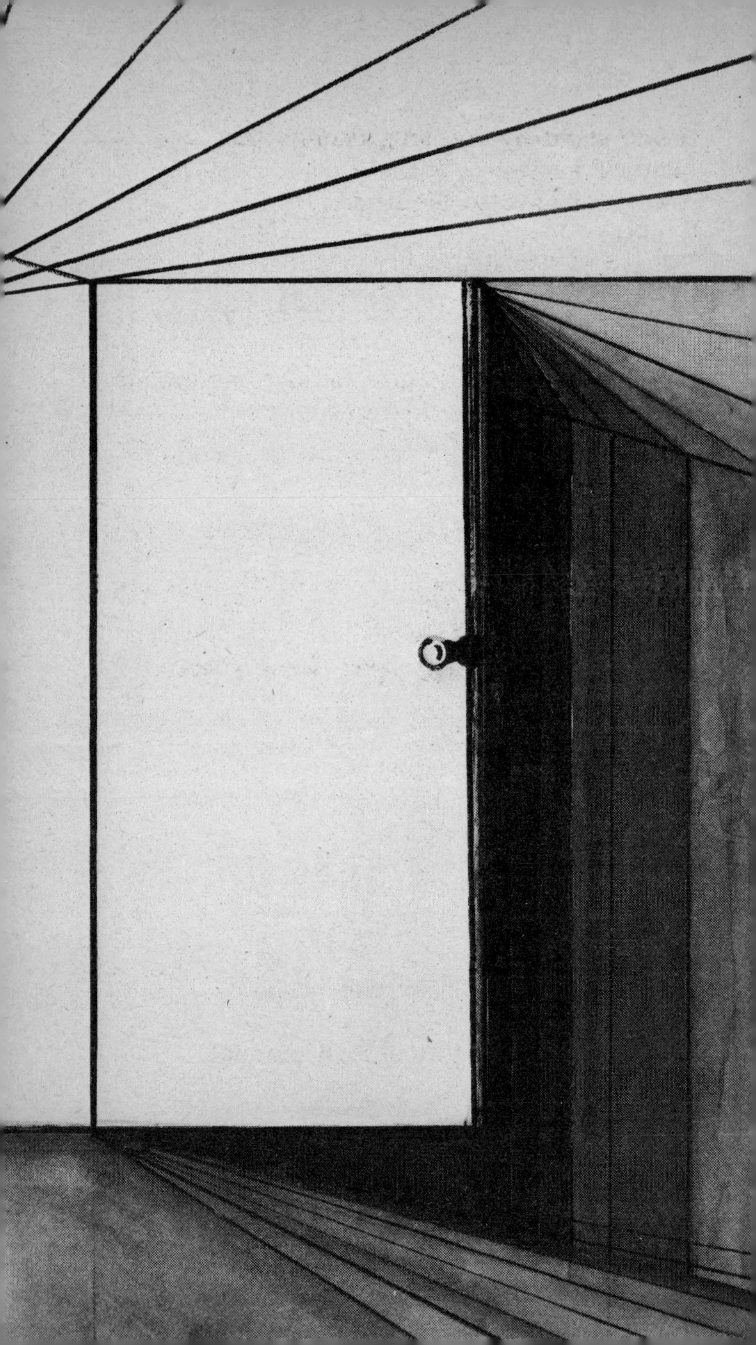

I will stand by you long enough that
you will know
you don't have to be afraid.
I mean
REALLY KNOW."

The fear all of us experience when contemplating
letting someone inside.
Fear arising from the dismal, doubting swamp of
If you REALLY knew who I was you
would leave me all alone
and I would fall.
Listen to me —
you REALLY don't have to be afraid!

That is an open door.
But you see
to walk through that open door is not
free.
It is open but
expensive.
To enter you must do battle with demons.
Those horrid demons of,
"but I am a bad girl"
of
"Do you think he would mind?"
of
"is it a sin that will put me in hell?"

We must be willing to at least examine
our freedom,
to let another know us
trusting
they will not run away in horror.
We must surrender.

We are so good at sharing strengths —
rather poor at sharing weaknesses.
We are taught to be weak
is to admit you are weak.
So we don't.
So we die in our pseudo strength.

No, rather than that most of us would rather
crash into a brick wall.
A thousand times over we confirm our certitude
"no one really cares FOR ME,"
"I must be strong and let no one know,"
"I must give with no thought of allowing others
to give to me."
Brick walls all.
With bloody head and broken hearts
we back off
get another good run
and do it again.

Hopefully few who read these lines
are in a place where
there is no one who loves and would allow
us to love them —
who is denied any open door.
For most of us it is much more a question of
will we choose the open door,
demon-guarded though it be.
Would we rather continue in our
headlong dash into untrusting giving
than
walk in love with another through the
door of relationship.

It is such a staggering thought that,
scientists tell us,
we actualize only about 10% of our potential.
That means we see but 10% of what is there,
hear but 10% of the world's music,
touch but 10% of this marvelously blessed globe's
riches.
And if this is true of the physical senses it is
more true
of our spiritual capacities.
We actualize only about 10% of our capacity
to grasp the meaning of
BODY OF CHRIST.

In love the Redeemer came to us,
in love he stands eager as the open door
to allow all to enter,
but where are we?
If we hear and come
how can it be that the world,
our world,
is so glutted with Jans and Caseys
and even beautiful little Beccys who
think they are bad.
Have we not all repeatedly broken the
Bread of the Eucharist?
Have we not countless times heard and said
BODY OF CHRIST?

We know what it is,
every child exposed to any Christian doctrine
KNOWS WHAT IT *IS*
perhaps we have yet far to go in grasping
what it means!

2

EUCHARIST AS FAITH

There is a trap hidden in this chapter title.
Of course Eucharist demands faith.
What is not so "of course" is
just what is this faith in Christ
as Eucharist?
Again, it is a question of
meaning.

What, to you, is the meaning of the
reality of Christ?

We have a tendency to
crash into Christ
as we do into most other things.
We have so little time to
let things be,
to reflect,
to sit quietly by the temple of any reality
and wait for the doors to open
under reverence
rather than yield to force.
We approach so much like mechanics
if not outright pirates
rather than poets.
If we are not to
crash into Christ
we must pay the price of
reverent waiting.

If we are ever to know more of what
BODY OF CHRIST
means we must quietly ask to be led.

In John Courtney Murray's classic book
THE PROBLEM OF GOD
he clearly shows how the basic problem of
the ancient Jew
was always one of presence and power.

"Are you here?
And if you are, do you have the power to
make any difference?"

All of this and more is fundamentally included
in Moses' basic question to God,
"What is your name?"

Many of modern man's basic questions
of faith
are also aimed at the presence and power of God.
However,
perhaps there is also a vastly other
vital consideration in
modern man's question of faith.

I suspect there are countless believers who
throng our Churches who have no
abiding question as to the
presence and power of God.
Not even to his basic benevolence.
By all means God is a good God,
by all means he wishes good to man —
but I'm not so sure he wills it
FOR ME.

Like little Beccy —
or big Jan,
or in between, Casey,
countless of our brothers and sisters are caught
in the grind of
faulty religious education
(which leaves us feeling constantly like
ugly sinners unworthy of God's love)
coupled with sick manipulation by Madison Ave.
(which would have us believe we are NEVER
young enough, beautiful enough or smart
enough.)

I suspect there are huge throngs that would
readily admit, my wife deserves the best from
God,
my husband is a living saint,
my kids aren't perfect but surely
good kids
who deserve a break from God.
But ME,
no, I don't deserve a good thing from God.

Most of us are good lovers
but
terrible at allowing ourselves to
be loved:
we are generous to a fault in
giving to others
but have scant skill or courage in
receiving.

The tragedy is that all too often
this frame of mind gets tagged
virtue.

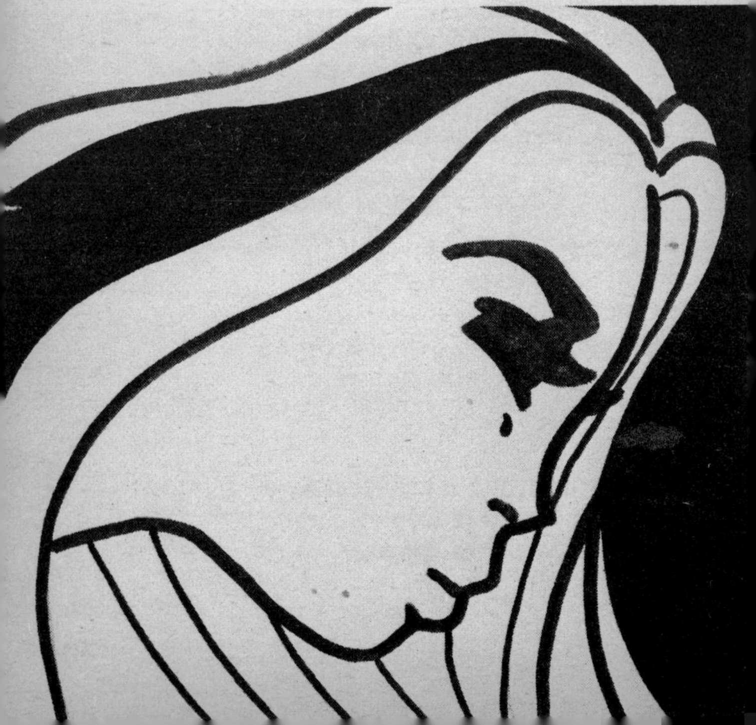

Under that banner
there is nothing more to do but
get more of it.
And under that tragic mind set we
quite effectively lock Christ out.

Who is your Christ?

We get so tied up in our own cultural traps
we lose sight of the fact that
the core of religion is not basically concerned with
our giving.
It is not basically dealing with how good we can
be.
The core of this way of life called
Christian is
that Christ is God's gift to us.
The primary question of our religion is
will we accept the gift?
Will we allow ourselves to
be loved?

Jesus
is the open door.
What we are asked to do —
despite all the demons —
is to stop running into brick walls.

It is such a different and
more difficult thing
in faith
to shift from the intellectual level
of presence and power
and deal with the personal question of
accepting that we are loved by God.

We are his people.
His beloved.

On the intellectual level we can assent
to God's presence and power
and have it change our lives not at all.
Something like discovering that there is a new
nebula in the galaxy somewhere.
Marvelous but
after all — so what?

There is no such powerlessness however
in the question of faith as to
our lovability in God's eyes.

Perhaps no one fully knows
all the elements that diminish modern man,
Americans,
but there seems to be such an
epidemic of guilt feelings,
so much loneliness, alienation and loss of meaning,
such an abundance of facades to cover up
the real question:
Can I love and be loved —
and the question of faith:
Will I accept I am loved
BY God?

THE NEW WAY

There is a New Way brought to man
by God in Christ.

The new way
of a benevolent God.

Have we heard it,
bought into it?

Who is your Christ?

The new way is one of acknowledgment.
It is a certitude that
God loves me
and what happens is or can be turned into
my growth.
God does not,
will not,
want to break us
and leave us broken.

We all know that in our heads.
It is not to be presupposed that we
know it in our hearts.
Crashing into Christ and
religion
as we often do
we might not even be aware if we have considered
this primary question of Christianity
or not.

Keith
is one of the holiest,
most Christ centered men I have
ever met.
You'd think there never could be a
question of faith in his life.
Obviously he believes so much
his whole life is a prayer of
compassion and verbalized Christianity.
Yet
he does struggle with a faith question.
Not as to God's power or presence,
nor even to his love FOR OTHERS,
but of his love for Keith.

It was winter and Keith
needed boots.
He lives in a prayer community that
offers up all needs
to the Lord.

There is no question
in general
of God's love for the community.
He always comes through.
Always!
But Keith found it hard to
accept
that God would want HIM to have boots.
Everyone else —
yes,
but not him.

And perhaps there is no
deeper question of faith,
for any of us,
than our acceptance of
God's love for us.

That God turns a benevolent face upon the
universe
many will accept.
That he turns such a benevolent face
upon me
is another question.

But Jesus has come to offer
a new way.
One that tells us that
God loves us.

Our Christian churches are
full
of charitable activity.

So countless many profit from
meals on wheels,
St. Vincent DePaul,
The Legion of Mary,
Big Brother and Sister programs —
the list of organized groups is almost endless.

Never to be known is the
unorganized,
miracle-producing activity of
other apostles of love.
Hospitals visited,
aged given rides,
shut-ins who have someone drop in just to
talk a bit.

At the big times of Christmas and Easter
every institute in the land is filled
with choirs, well-wishers and
volunteers who reach out a hand that
others may have a hand to hold.

Certainly most of these would
give God credit.
Who would doubt that God
wanted the sick visited,
the shut-ins befriended,
the orphans taken on picnics.

Wonderful.

What is not so wonderful is if we allow
our image of God
to leave us parked outside after the
last passenger has been let off.

It is not so good,
certainly not virtuous,
to allow God to be
FOR US
someone who simply uses us to
enhance the lives of others.

God does not want primarily
for us to be used
even by Him
for the growth of someone else.
If we are to accept the
image of a loving Father
and a loving Good Shepherd then we must,
regardless of the courage needed,
work our way through all our demons to
accept that God loves me
FOR ME
not just for how he can use me.

Certainly we are to be used
to be Sacraments as He is
Sacrament
for the illumination of the World.

But just as Christ was never
separated from the
love of the Father
so neither must we be.

But my how fear
gets in the way.
We fear when things don't go right because
maybe God is mad at me.
We fear when they do because
I'm sure he will take it away.
As one man said,
"I'm afraid he is setting me up for a fall."
We are so sure
everyone else deserves the love of God —
but not me.
And so we don't let go.
We repeatedly choose the wall.

Back at the turn of the century
Clarence Darrow wrote a most moving story
about a poverty stricken Jewish boy.
It was winter in Darrow's story
and the waif constantly hung around the
glamorous downtown stores.
He loved to look in the windows
behind which stood so many lovely things.
Things he wanted passionately for his mother.
Under Darrow's compassionate, sensitive hand
you can almost feel the bitter cold wind
as it wrapped itself around the boy,
you can feel the dreams dance in his head
as he looks at the merchandise
for others.
You can feel the resignation,
the "I deserve it"
as the store manager shoos him away from the
window.

Many perhaps would claim not to identify
with this boy.
Most certainly do not feel themselves
standing outside a rich store window
looking in.
But don't we?

What else do we make of ourselves
when we are so sure that others deserve
God's gifts,
just about any others —
but not us.
What else are we when that rush of
embarrassment or guilt or
false humility sweeps over us when we are
confronted
deeply
by one who tells us,
"Hey, God really loves you."
Doesn't the image of that poor
deprived waif
ring true
every time we agree that
"God got even" if
something should go wrong.
And on a far deeper, more essential level
if we are to meet the living,
loving God —
a level perhaps we have yet to ask questions
about —
how certain are we that God is
leading us on,
leading us to the joy and peace promised by
the Good news.

How certain are we that He never takes away
without giving back what is better.

BODY OF CHRIST.
Only God could keep count of all the times
that has been, is and will be said.
But what does it mean?
Who is this Christ
whose Body we seek communion with?
What does He want?
What is His stance toward us?
Where is He leading us?

Abraham thought he knew.
He didn't especially want to be a prophet,
to lead his people.
Continually he asked to be shown where
he was being led.
No doubt,
much like us,
he was willing to make sacrifices.
Even hard ones.
He was willing to give up what he wanted
and where he was secure,
even his home.
He would engage a long, uncertain, dusty trip
if that was what God asked.
It might not make much sense but
if that was what God wanted,
he would do it.
But as surely as night follows day
there came that terrifying moment,
that moment of faith —
that "time" when *all* was asked.

It was a question of faith,
real faith.
Not faith in "some" God somewhere
or to this God's power.
It was a question as to whether this God
was for him or not.
Abraham, as most of us,
tended to always keep a back door open.
"I'll give you what I can handle.
Even if it's hard I'll give you what you want
as long as
it isn't everything."
But God is a surgeon.
His concern is with the diseased part.
Like a true arrow he sought out Abraham's most
treasured possession, his son.

Now either God is basically
primarily FOR US,
each of us,
or he is not.
If he is then anything he asks is for
OUR GOOD
not just his amusement.
If he is not basically for us,
loves us,
then by all means —
keep that back door open.
God just might come at us
then
in a bad mood or with some pretty sick
humor,
take away what seems so precious to us
just for fun and giving
nothing back.

It is a question of faith.
Radical faith.
Will this God play with me
like a fish on a hook —
or —
are we gold in his pan.

If we don't ask the question,
which we can't if we don't face it
then we don't know.

Without consciously being aware of it
perhaps
many who weekly (or even daily) witness the
BODY OF CHRIST
lifted up within the people
really suspect he just might
snatch our crutches away without giving us
something better.

He just might leave us at the brick wall
and never open the door
FOR US.

Very possibly we never think of it in those
rather harsh terms
but that nagging suspicion that
"I'm really not worth it" or
"God can't REALLY love me" persist.

We break our necks for others
but are not so sure that God
(or perhaps anyone else)
would do as much for us.

And who could blame them.
Receiving demands such a courageous
way-to-be in this world.
Especially from God.

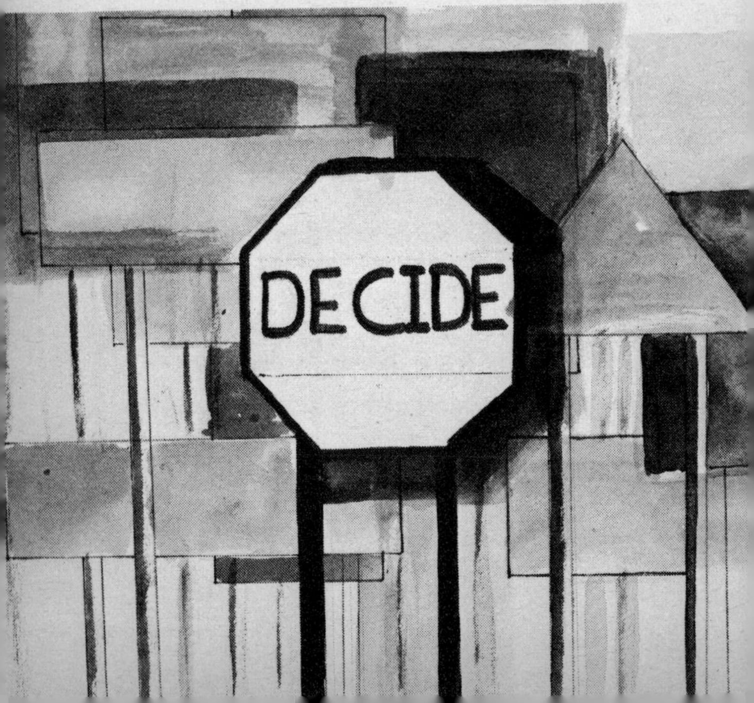
DECIDE

As with Abraham
be assured to hear the name of God
is to hear the surgeon approaching our
disease of slavery.
Whatever it might be.

That which we think we
cannot do without,
that mask we most need
for a hiding place
surely
God won't ask of us —
he will pluck away.

But not exactly pluck away.
God did not raise the knife over
Isaac,
Abraham did.

God asks us to hand over
freely
that which seems to wound us most.

For one it is an attachment to another,
for another it is attachment to self,
to one's own power or
the refusal to attach to anything;
it might be a letting go of a penchant for
being right, or being a clown, or being rich.

Just as there is almost every possible way of
being free
so there is every complex way of being
a slave.

The surgeon would set us free.

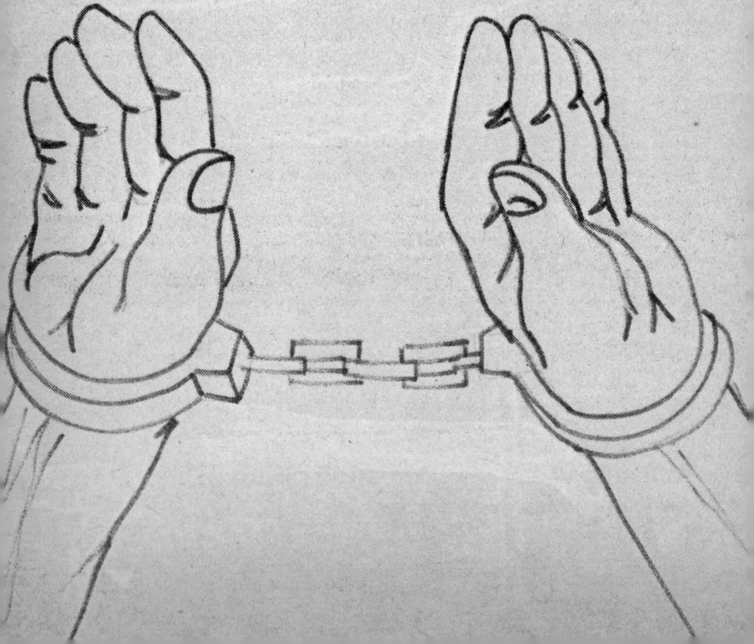

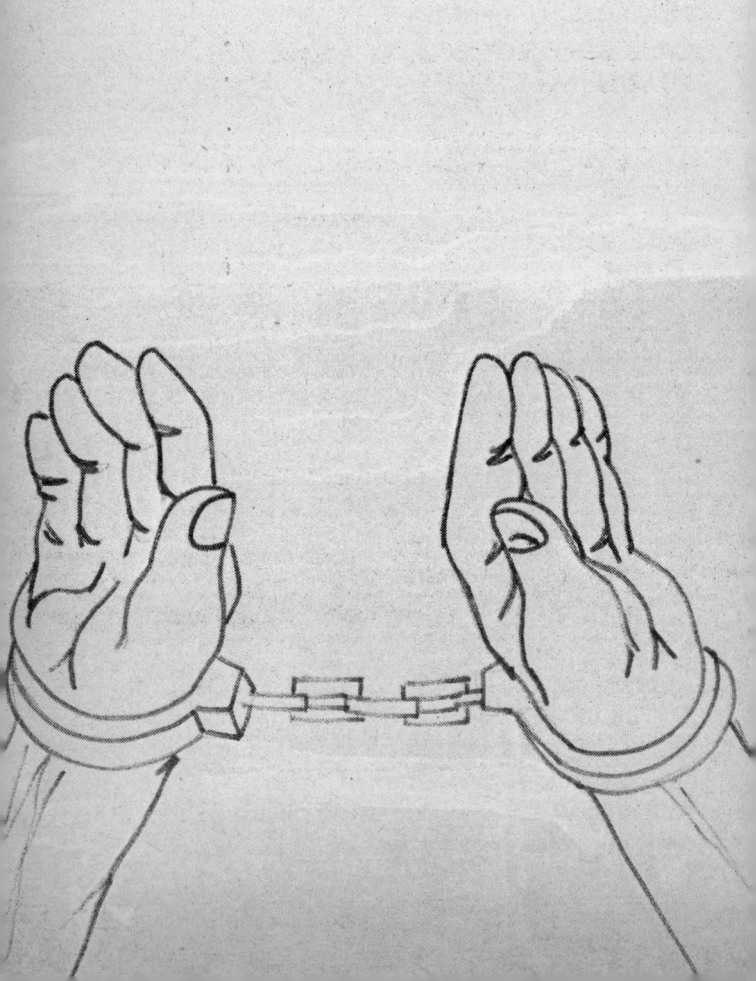

And always on the bottom line,
at the bottom of the pile is a question
of faith.

Not just can God take what he wants
or ask for what he wants —
but will we believe that it is
FOR OUR GOOD.
Will we accept that we are the
total recipients of God's infinite love.
That God is FOR US.

Many people are incredible at what they can
endure.
Pain can become a test of love.
They say,
"Let me show you how much I love you
by hurting for you."
True, love may ask much pain
but endurance without the acceptance of
love,
that we are loved
is an insult to the beloved.

Who in the world wants those we love
to be in pain
for the sake of pain!
Certainly not God.

Eucharist as Christ is
the question of our faith in Christ.
And that is the question of our courage in
accepting that we are loved.

Is anything ever new?
Isaiah the prophet is filled with
these same questions.

In his time the people of God forsook trust in him,
not in his power but in his willingness to
be good to them
and sought help from the Egyptians against
their enemies.

His Chapter 30 paints the picture of the people
fleeing to Egypt with
gifts and hope.
He shouts
trust and hope in "do nothing Egypt" will
avail them nothing.
Egypt seems strong but
has no real power.
Only in God is there power.

Without trust in God
he says
they will be destroyed,
there will be no joy or tranquility in their lives.

Then the marvelous,
contemporary lines spring out,

"For thus says the Lord Yahweh, the Holy One
of Israel:
Your salvation lay in conversion and tranquility,
your strength in complete trust,
and you would have none of it."

He then continues in words that sound like today,

"No" you said, "We will flee on horses."
So be it, flee then!
And you add, "In swift chariots."
So be it, your pursuers will be swift too.

And so we run to Egypt.
We mount our "swift horses" of
wisdom, strength or ability to
endure
to substitute for the open door.
But it can't.
It doesn't.

Only God is God.
The God who in faith
asks us to accept
that he is for us.
Before all, in all and behind all
he is for us.

BODY OF CHRIST!

3

EUCHARIST AS HEALING

*As the Father was
made present in his Sacrament,
Jesus,
so Jesus is made present
in his living Sacraments —
us.
Christians are the Sacraments of the
living God.
We are called upon to
heal one another
in the name and power of Jesus.*

Every week I spot Ed at Mass,
always in the back row.

Ed is big and successful,
he is young and handsome
and no dummy.

In any age Ed would have been a
successful merchant,
in any age he would have been the thoroughly
contemporary man.

Ed almost never goes to
communion.

He sits there with his wife and
lovely kids,
they go.
That makes him happy.

But not him, he
never comes forward.

Partly Ed is greatly trapped in the
"I don't deserve it" trap
but also he never got beyond the
"What it is" question to
what it means.

The physical presence has been stressed
to the exclusion of any spiritual presence.
That Eucharist could mean
growth,
love and trust,
that it could mean the pledge of God's
with-us-in-love,
I'm sure,
has never entered his mind,
let alone his heart.

There is no connection between Eucharist
and all the Jans, Caseys and Beccys
in his life.
One is of heaven — unearthly,
the other is very much of this earth — material.

Ed considers himself very much
of this earth.
He will and does
extend many loving hands to those in need,
he is a man who cares,
who agonizes over others' pain;
he is deeply in love with his family
He would very much want healed
in him
that which tears him apart.

And as always
it goes by the name of fear.

For all of his self-confidence,
assurance, wonderful appearance, there is so
much he is afraid of.
There is
so much he wants to be.

I suspect there are a great many Eds
in our community,
probably in yours as well.
Some, like Ed, may shun the table of the Lord,
others regularly approach.
But whether they do or not
there is no connection in their consciousness
between Eucharist,
fear they hate, and the
light they seek.

They would be healed
but Eucharist doesn't mean
healing
to them.

Jesus heals.
Only God can heal.
But what does Christ mean?
Who is he to us?
What is the BODY OF CHRIST?

As the Father was
made present in his Sacrament,
Jesus,
so Jesus is made present
in his living Sacraments —
us.

Christians are the Sacraments of the
living God.

We are called upon to
heal one another
in the name and Power of Jesus.

To do that we must be visible,
conscious Christians.

But just what is a
Visible Christian?

Again, due to our culture,
we tend to
crash into this question.

Most of us would probably connect
Visibility primarily with
activity.
Mostly a matter of doing.
"If
we are going to
heal someone
let's get busy and do it!"

Healers heal.
Healers are not first of all
doers.

They are first of all and
primarily, always,
those who have walked with God,
who have stopped to listen,
who allow his Power to stream out
that the frozen may be warmed
and the dark made light.

Is it simply my goodness
or yours
that keeps you from suicide,
Casey from an institution,
or Beccy from the slum of
self doubt.

Do we heal or
is it God through us.

And if God
then
the Power of his gift is that
He has loved us,
called us His own,
sent us His Spirit.

And we are as
powerful to heal others
as we have
allowed ourselves to be healed!

The Visible Christians,
in some mysterious way,
are first of all those who have
allowed themselves
to be broken by God,
who have given the gift of
Abraham
and surrendered to the
awful terror of the
open door.

Healing,
or ministry,
does not come from our
strength of wholeness
but from our
weakness made strength
through being lovingly,
if painfully,
broken by the Lord.

Gentleness heals.
Many an iron door
of fear
that no Hun could break
has timidly slid open
under the gentle tapping
of a small hand.

In God's own time,
which is always the right time
for us,
the Word of God comes
as hunter
to our door.

He comes seeking his
ruthless exchange —
our strength for His,
our wisdom for His,
our cross for His.
Perhaps it is an inch
at a time,
sometimes more,
but the Word is ever there.

Not only history
and the story of great Saints
are filled with
fighting the Word —
resisting the elemental faith question
of God's love for us.
Personally —
so do each of our lives
give testimony to the eternal struggle.

"God"
we cry out in our own way,
"I will gladly remain
a cripple!
Leave me my crutches.
Please,
anything,
but don't ask me to give up my
hiding place.
I have been there so long,
I know it well.
I am comfortable there."

The trade
and Hunter are
ruthless.
Only healers can heal.
Jesus would have us whole
for our own sake —
but also that we may build up
The Body of Christ.

We sat in a group
as we do every week,
some 15 men, before work,
before dawn has broken.
Each
in his own limited, limping way
would be made whole.
Each
fighting his own demons
we break through the open door
to meet our God.
We seek to be
Visible Christians
not by doing charitable, noticed
activity
but by allowing ourselves to be
healed by God,
to be caught in his net.

Sooner or later
each of us
will be asked the gift of Abraham.
If we resist
it will be asked again,
then again,
and again
until we die or
it is given.
If it is not given before
we die
God surely will be sad
for
we will have cheated ourselves of
much of His Joy and Power.

From thousands of throats,
in thousands of hands
the Eucharist —
Body of Christ.

Tens of thousands of eyes
turn to look up.
Some are sleepy,
some full of doubt
or apathy or fear or
curiosity.

Some full of the
light of God,
of confidence and commitment
of being healed that
healing may flourish.

That which is familiar and easy often runs
such terrible risk of
death by routine.
We take it for granted.
Even
The Body of Christ.

Ryan gathers with us weekly.
Like all of us his name is
Abraham.
When Ryan is most in need,
when he is most hurt,
most vulnerable, most lonely,
he "plays the quiet game."
He clams up.

He refuses to give the gift of
vulnerability,
of trust,
to those he loves.

Ryan says he just
endures.
In due time the need
passes.

He recovers and
can once again assume his
customary
in control role of giver.

But
the greatest gift he has
already refused to give.

Ryan is a good man,
a just man.
With all his heart he would
heal others.
He would wish the Power of Christ
to flow through him that
others may be able to share
their pain and
be healed.

He knows
no more precious gift could
anyone give him
than the trust of sharing their fear.
But he
cannot share his.

And the Hunter is
at his door, nagging.

Each week,
every week,
something is said that indicates
his struggle within.

Abraham
is being asked to surrender
that weakness may become
strength
that others may be healed as well.

John is so painfully
shy.
Who knows what tapes
whirr within,
what thoughts of perhaps
being nothing good enough to say.
But he comes,
each week,
while the hunter stalks without.
I suspect John could find
many reasons for not coming
or dropping out.
But there is also one
compelling reason
for sticking in;
God asks him to.

At times you can almost hear
the conversation,
"Lord,
leave me alone!

I'll go to Mass,
pray in private,
be a generous Christian,
but leave me alone.
Don't ask me to go
in a group
and share my faith.
What if they laugh!
What if it isn't wise,
too silly."

But how is John to discover
the beauty of his faith,
the depth of his wisdom
if he does not speak it forth.

And if he does not
taste this joy of the Lord
how shall he be this
Visible Christian
who will have the power
of his surrender
to free others.

Brad is new
He is a loving marshmallow
incased in a salty shell.
Brad doesn't know about
Abraham yet,
but he will.
As sure as there is a God
he will —
and he will fight like a
netted shark.

In Brad's mind he is a
sinner.
Repentant, yes —
but so many sins that
surely
God could never really forget.

I suspect Brad
has no doubt whatever
how much God loves Father Larsen,
John and Ryan —
all the group —
but not him.

After all the group
doesn't know his track record, —
God does.
He loves the group.
No doubt he sees himself as
taker, not giver.
For all he's done, now
in the autumn of his life,
perhaps it isn't too late to
make up
for some of his sins.

Beware, Brad!
He comes like a thief in the
night.
Perhaps first in a whisper or
maybe a storm,
but your place of hiding,
your most tightly locked door
will be knocked upon.

Like the rest of us
you will be asked to surrender,
to embrace that which you
fear most.

Through the gate of
willingness to listen, God
will ask you to accept that,
sinner, as we all are,
he loves you.

He will ask you to
step from behind the
prohibitive shield of felt
unworthiness
to gaze upon His loving face
A face not only loving toward
"them"
but you.

Perhaps like the rest of us
you will fight,
you will kick and thrash and scream —
but you will not escape.
The Lord seeks to
break you,
to take away your defense,
to break your wall.

You
are so high and enthused about
the group now
but I don't think
the gift of Abraham
has been asked of you yet.

You will be sorry you ever came —
and never so glad.
The Body of Christ will
never be the same.
Did the Lord not
break you
how would you ever have the power
to heal.

Dick is smart.
He has always been smart.
It has always been important
to have right answers.
Dick needs an orderly world
made of orderly, predictable parts.
His was a solid world of
problem and answer
not mystery and journey when
nothing is certain
God leads us on.
Nothing but that the
gift of Abraham will be
asked
and the joy and power of Abraham
will be won if
the gift be surrendered.
That was Dick's world.
No more.
He heard the knock and
opened the door.
There stood God with a
stone knife and
the son of Dick's slavery
asking it be put to death.

Dick doesn't have to be right any more,
he just has to be on the way.
Nor must the world be predictable
because
Dick has relinquished control of it.
Who is to say if
Ryan's sharing need is more
painful
than John's sharing of self is
razor edged?
Who knows if Brad's
yet to be made exchange
will cost him more than
Dick has paid?
Who knows?
What does it matter?
We each are Abraham.
We each walk with our Isaac.

Only healers heal.
Eucharist is Christ and
Christ has come that the world may have
abundant life.
Within the Body of Christ
is abundant Life —
for within the Body
Abraham has raised the knife
over Isaac,
slavery is being
put to death that Life
may stand forth.

Dick no longer has to have
the right answer
and Ryan at least knows what
is asked of him and
where the door is.

Nor am I an idle
observer,
as with all of us my
Isaac walks at my side.
The Hunter ruthlessly pursues me
as well.
I have left my share of blood
on the brick wall beside the
open door.
Most fearful of all is
the risk to need,
to expect,
to depend on others.
What in the world if
they don't come through?
Alone
I can endure —
the journey can be made —
But not made,
if I listen
as He wants.

To need no one is
not to need God.

Not to need God is
to rely on my own power —
which is never enough.

Not only not enough
to do,
it most certainly is not enough
to be,
to change,
to grow,
to trust.

And so as the others,
in due season
the sacrifice is asked.
As with the others I ask,
I beg,
leave me alone!
I'll do your work.
I'll preach your word,
comfort your sick,
touch your broken people.
I'll visit your jails,
answer night calls,
baptize your babies,
put up with your kooks.
Leave me alone.
What else do you want!
I know what He wants.
I hear it as plainly as the
silence in this room, —
I hear it in the silence.
"I want you."

"Not what you can
or cannot do,
or *think* you can do,
or cannot do.

What do you know what
you can or can't do till
you allow yourself to be
healed.
Till then
it is your word you speak
not mine.
I would have you speak
my word.
But you cannot do that
till you let me have
you."

Never again will the
Body of Christ
be the same.
Not for me.
Not for anyone who would
listen,
who would be open to the
open door.

And Sunday I will see Ed.
I wish he were
healed.
I wish he would hear
Body of Christ.

But only Jesus heals.
He loves Ed more than I.
He comes to Ed in his own way,

I will leave Ed
up to Him.

4

EUCHARIST AS DIALOGUE

"Logos" means "word."
Jesus is the Logos of God.
"Dia-" is a Greek prefix
meaning "apart."
You and I have our roots
unbreakably sunk
in the Logos.
We are separate, apart,
yet facing one another
rooted in Jesus who
is our being.

A lady I dearly love recently
gave birth to a baby.
It was a long, dangerous pregnancy
and the birth would be the same.
During her first few months everything
was secret —
no one must know,
no one be worried.

She and God would handle this,
thank you,
no one else was especially needed.
It would be frightening and hard
but she would make it,
she would endure.

God visited this lovely woman
in His mysterious way.
Abraham laid down Isaac.

Upon returning home after
a trip
I called her.

Despite much physical pain
and doubt as to the
unborn baby's health
she was radiant —
"I feel so close
to God,"
she said,
"so incredibly close to God.
And the reason is because I am so
absolutely certain he
loves me."

It is God who heals,
God who gives joy.

But I asked her if
people had come through
for her.
Silence.
Over the phone I could see —
she was shaking her head,
in amazement.
She often has lately.
The silence was not an indication of
a negative response —
it was the sound
of having too much to say!

Geri
had brought over meals,
Dorothy had come to
vacuum and do laundry,
Mary had kept in constant touch,
so many had called.

God is God
no matter who or what man is.

But man is the
Sacrament,
the show-through
of God.

God is not God
to man
without man!

God would not have been
the same
to this fine woman
without her friends enfolding her
in love and concern.

We need human dialogue
to enter into divine communion.

We need the experience of human
absolution
to feel God's forgiveness,
human love
to know Infinite love,
human trust
to find the open door who
is God.

This certainly is not new
or surprising.

But for all of that
for all we hear from
".....ologists" of every kind
telling us of the nature and
necessity of
dialogue in relationship and
notwithstanding the growing impact of
Marriage Encounter with their emphasis on
dialogue.
Many indeed have yet to find this
key to God.

Fewer still perhaps
have heard the reality of dialogue
within the meaning of Eucharist.

As with the experience of the
pregnant woman
most of us have discovered that
as our own freedom emerges
so does Christ emerge in our lives.

Jesus is for us,
for our freedom and joy
in the deepest sense of those words.
Therefore to meet the Lord
always has tied with it
the experience of freedom.

As Christ emerges
so do we emerge
for in Christ is the power
not only to be who we want
but to be able to do what is most
deeply human.

Eucharist is love.
Love is dialogue.
Dialogue is the fruit and root of relationship.
It happens in the space between.

Love is not something we have
like marbles in our pocket
but the name of a creative power
existing between lover and the
beloved.

Victor Frankle in his method of
human healing called Logotherapy repeats the
importance of what he calls participation.

If there is to be meaning
in our lives
there must be participation of one
with another.

Senility
he says
is often little more than loss of
meaning in life due to
lack of participation with others.

The aged are set in some corner
or room or institution —
participation is cut off.
No sharing, no dialogue.
No one takes an interest any more.

The fire of their diamonic
burns lower and lower,
finally simply sputtering out.

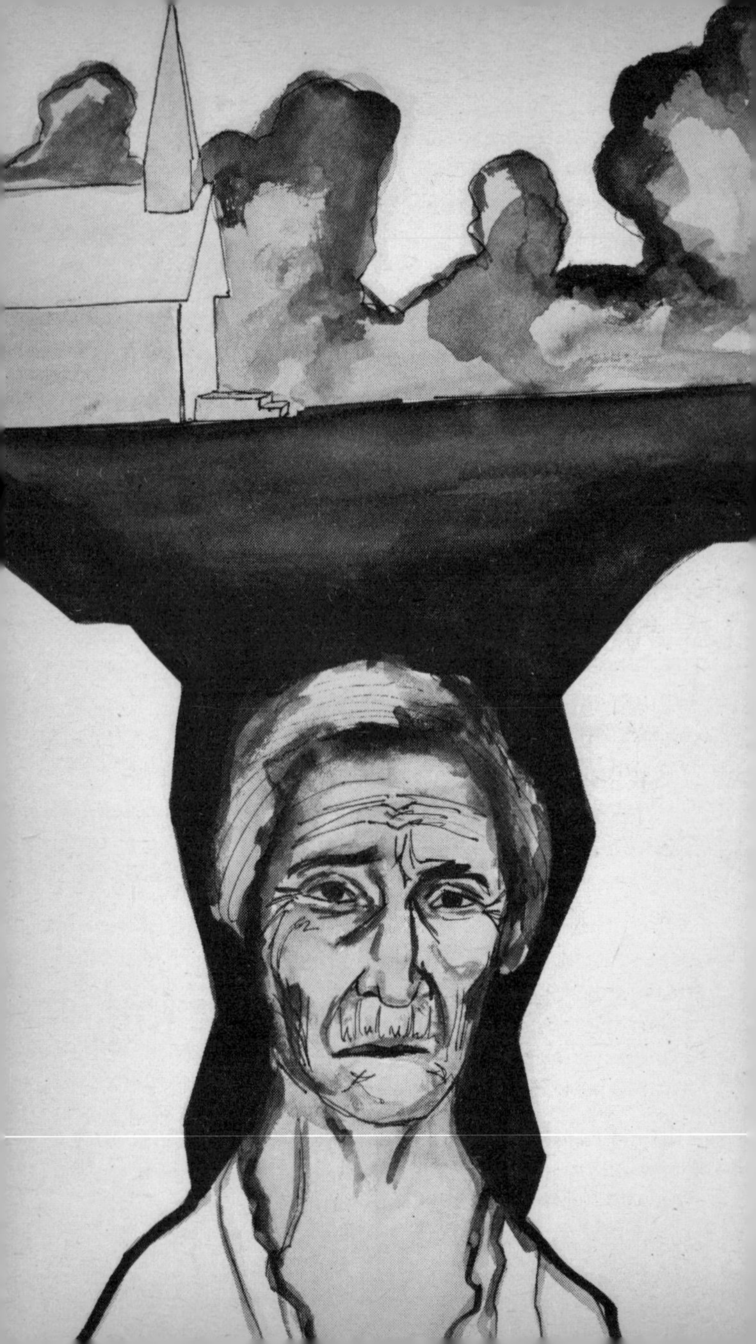

Dr. William Glasser gives no less
importance to dialogue
in his method of health and healing called
reality therapy.
His word for dialogue is
involvement.
There simply can be no healing of the
broken
he says, without involvement.
We don't want someone
with cold analytical shrewdness to
tell us what is wrong with us.
What we need is someone to walk with us,
to wisely care for us,
to be gentle with our weakness,
to offer a hand that together we may face
the terror of the open door.
Advice,
even good advice
without involvement is always
futile he says.

Always.

When the Lord comes
awhispering to Big Ed
inviting him to communicate in
Eucharist
Ed will probably try to fight, squirm
and no doubt go it alone.

The first reaction is always to
go it alone.
Me and God.

But the Hunter never lets go.
Sooner or later it always leads to
communion with others.
We don't go through the open door
alone.
All the sage advice in the world
isn't what Ed is seeking.
Or will seek,
or alone needs.
Sooner or later he will seek another.
And that someone will be a
visible Christian.
Visible not for what they do or
the amount they do
but visible for their depth.
A depth dug out by the Lord when the
letting go was begun.

Glasser has this rugged
but wise
summary of the rules in helping another
in dialogue,
"... you must never give up or give in."

Jesus of course was before
Buber, May, Frankle or Glasser.
He was speaking dialogue,
freedom,
religion when he said,
"Love me as I have loved you."
We do not live in a vacuum,
grow in a vacuum,
find freedom alone,
we do not get sick alone nor
are we healed alone.

Our spirits feed on dialogue as our
bodies on food
and our lungs on air.
And if not Jesus or
any of the others let us take the testimony
of our own hearts.

When finally beaten down and ready to
surrender,
when we have kissed our concrete, have we never
reached out to another simply saying,
"I have to talk to you.
I am starving.
Allow me the food of
dialogue."

At the moment of considered suicide
Jan didn't need or ask for advice.
Only dialogue,
the being present of one person with another
would keep her from taking
her life
and perhaps someone else's.
Not just dialogue in word
but in compassion and understanding,
in truth and honesty.

The presence of those qualities,
those ways of being present to one another
was sealed in prayer.

That prayer moved her to tears,
indicating that a raw nerve is as
touched
as Eucharist is meant to touch
raw nerves.

Whatever Casey is going to do
or become
will depend on his luck and courage
in finding dialogue.
He may well earn his way into a
mental institution.
He may perish there.
If not it will be because he found a
group
or someone
with whom he could dialogue.
And in walking that
space between
find out he is not all alone.
That it is O.K. to be Casey.
That he doesn't have to play games
or seek escape in death of one kind or another.

It isn't enough to just tell him that.
Telling him is the
door to the temple of God-on-earth.
He needs to go through that door.
He needs to get on the inside of that
window,
no longer being a frozen waif
standing all alone on the outside.

Beccy
as she grows
will hear over and over,
God loves you,
her parents will tell her
and do
love her without limit.

But even now —
so young —
she needs to taste and see,
to touch and hear and sense that
you bet your life
I am gold in someone else's pan!

Without that she,
like the rest of us,
wanders around in the land of
maybe.

Maybe I am O.K.,
maybe I am good enough,
maybe someone could love me.

And even to have the freedom to ask
that question
is a sign of life.
So many of our frozen brothers and sisters
can't even do that.

DIA-LOGUE

Even the root meaning of the word
"dialogue"
is a beautiful meditation in itself.

Logos
we have come to accept means
"word."
Jesus is the Logos of God.

It didn't mean that originally.
The ancient Greek philosopher,
Heraclitus,
uses the word in an entirely different way.

To him
(and he should know —
it is a Greek word) it
means something like
"collectedness."
It means "gathered together."
It has the feel of
"that out of which everything grows
and stands rooted."

Not rooted in the sense of
fixed or stationary
but rooted in that
it belongs.
It is the basic, primary, fundamental
level within which everything that is
exists.

Dia-
is a Greek prefix meaning
"apart."
Apart like
thrown apart.

If you have ever tripped when carrying a
bag of oranges
and seen them rolling away in every which way
you are looking at
"dia . . .".

Dia - logos
then is standing apart,
you and I standing apart in our
uniqueness,

I as me and
you as you
with no attempt to make you a shadow
of me, or me
be blotted up into you like spilled ink.

We retain our individual identity
and in fact seek to enhance that
separateness
for you can only be free
as you —
not as a copy of me.

But
we are rooted together in our
collectedness.
Our roots are unbreakably sunk
in the Logos.

We are separate, apart
yet facing one another
rooted in Jesus who is our
being.

The opposite of dia-logue is
dia-bolic.

Ballo is a Greek verb
simply meaning 'thrown."
In dia-bolic existence there is the same
dia-
the same separateness but no
collectedness.
There is then truly the
casting out where there is wailing and
the gnashing of teeth.

We are thrown apart with no hope of touching,
or standing together either in our own facing of one another,
nor
in the root level of our being.

There is no commonalty,
no coming together.

Syn-
is the prefix meaning the opposite of dia.

Syn- is to come together.
It means co-,
as in co-operation or
co-investment.

Or as St. Paul used it to be
co-crucified and so to co-rise with
the Logos who is Christ.

We use the word
sym-bolic
to mean thrown back together.
To live in unity.

Symbolic living is the
coming back together that
diabolic living
threw apart in darkness and fear.

Sym-bolically in dia-logue we
risk the invitation of
Abraham's gift and approach the
open door.

Isolated,
which all diabolic living is,
we simply wither away in our fear
and sin.

Jesus truly calls us to live in
dia-logue
to be rooted in him and with one another.

Jesus is the gift of God,
He who is Word,
seeking response that
we may be healed and thus
from our brokenness
be sources of strength and healing to others.

There are so many reasons why we find
dialogue so frightening.
The same reasons why we find love
frightening.

And more to the point why
we find accepting love
such an enormous task.

To truly enter into dialogue
demands that slowly,
as slowly as it need be,
we allow the revelation of who we are
to take place.

All those hidden locked doors
some perhaps we didn't even know existed
are approached and knocked upon.

So often we would
pass them by,
open all but "those"
yet we know somehow that our
freedom and best self is also
locked up behind those doors.

Father Powell in his fine book,
THE SECRET OF STAYING IN LOVE,
says that we can know no more of ourselves
than we will allow someone else to know.
But if we do not know ourselves
how can we ever march toward
progressive freedom.
And if we are not striving to be free
how can we worship the God who is
freedom itself.
God has not asked us to be slave,
but free.
And we are again deposited
right back to the fundamental question of
faith —
does God want freedom and joy
FOR ME?

BODY OF CHRIST!

How far we have come in our
reflections and meditations.

From a static, more or less dynamic
ritual of a man who is priest holding up a
piece of bread saying,
"Body of Christ"
and throngs filing up to
eat of the Bread
we have pounded on the door of
meaning.

A meaning that takes us to perhaps
unasked questions,
questions about open doors and terrifying
considerations of faith.

We have twined the meaning of Abraham's gift,
whatever Isaac might be,
with the Divine Hunter
who would break our slavery that
we might be healed and thus be
healers.

We have sat at the foot of ancient
pagan, Heraclitus,
and listened to the gentle words of Jesus
"love one another."

And when all is said and done
we have stood
looking out upon the ocean of dialogue,
at times turbulent and at others
compelling by its loveliness
but never routine.

But there comes a time when looking
out upon the ocean is simply not enough,
when the only thing that suffices is to
launch forth,
to live the poet's life,
to give the gift
that would set us free,
ourselves.

It is indeed terribly frightening to be
honest,
to meet ourselves in the brilliant
light of dialogue.
There is but one thing more
terrifying —
being dishonest.
For then we have given our lives over
into the power of
unnamed forces that go where they will.

Eucharist,
like God,
is a verb, not
a noun.
Eucharist happens.
It happens in the
heard invitation
to come as guest,
to share hospitality,
to see and be seen.
For in that marvelous event
of persons touching
in trust and respect
a new dimension is entered.

Always —
to be conscious guest
in the home of another
is to be open to learn,
it is to be sensitive to the
gift
of others.
And thus is grace born.

The Yacci Indians have
no word for grace.
So they use the word for
flower,
to mean grace.
A Yacci rosary is
a beautiful thing —
dark brown beads
leading to a connecting center
leading to a crucifix
beneath which hangs
a brilliant red
tassel.
The tassel is called in
Yacci the name for flower
or grace.

From Mary is
Christ,
from Christ is
grace
and grace is life,
among us.
New Life flowering from
the New Way.

Christ's way of
courageous gifting and
receiving of gifts
that we may be healed.
Flowing from Christ
the red flower of grace —
Jan's tears,
Casey's hope,
Beccy's fawn-like voice,
proclaims the Hymn of Life,
"I am gold in your pan."

Drift through the world tonight
on the wings of your mind —
how many gifts held out in love,
rejected or taken,
how many wounded hearts
enduring silently or
asking to be healed,
from how many ministers in
hut or castle,
alley or auditorium,
Church or prison,
does the fiery flower of grace
manifest itself in exultant
power —
asking to be born,
begging to be born.
Groaning,
as Paul says,
until creation becomes
complete.

But grace, too, is a
poet,
as all flowers.

It comes as guest
gently touching our brokenness
with no promise of
instant answer.

It only proclaims
that in a world often
cruel and hard
there is also beauty —
like a soft hand
to hold
on a cold, tired night.

It doesn't promise an end
to pain
only a certainty of healing.
Where slavery ruled,
freedom shall reign.

In prayer do we enter,
as poet-guests,
into the brokenness of
the other —
prayer the climate,
prayer of the door.

When our brokenness
touches theirs
the flower bursts into flame.

Then are we born.

And the verb
that is Eucharist
paints the horizon of our
consciousness
in all the pastel grandeur of
a sunset

Body of Christ —

Christ who is dialogue,

Christ who invites us to dialogue

Christ who is met through dialogue.

5

EUCHARIST AS GIFT

Real gifts are always spiritual.
They are sacramental.
A gift devoid of its spiritual meaning
is just a thing.
Love is not in general.
Nor is growth.
It is in particular.
As Eucharist is an in particular gift.

Gift giving is the most wonderful
event we humans can create —
but it is not easy to do.

Real gifts are always spiritual.
They are sacramental.

A gift devoid of its spiritual meaning
is just a thing.

Things aren't bad
but they are terrible insults
if meant to be channels of spiritual meaning
and have no spiritual power.

It is not so much what a thing is
as what it means.

The strangest things
can be gifts —
things even like
freckles
if for one they are
messengers of meaning
and for the other
the meaning-as-gift
is given.

I know a case where
this freckles-as-gift
is deeply true.
I know another where
a mink coat
was given as thing
and rejected as insult.

All authentic gift giving is spiritual,
made
a thousand times more full and fulfilling
when we understand just what is
being given.

But this takes dialogue;
we have to let one another know.
We have to be willing to allow the other
to know who we are
if we are ever to have them understand
what it is we really give.

Full gift giving demands dialogue and
the courage to receive
For real gifts are always a testimony
to our power and importance in someone's
life.

I hope I never forget the closing scene
in the movie
THE HEART IS A LONELY HUNTER.
The healer who would not
be healed
and thus ended his life in suicide
left behind many people who could
have gifted him.
But it was too late.
The cynical, bitter Black doctor,
the teenage girl who had been given so
much in the gift of sensitivity and love
were both by his grave.
It was too late.
Why, they wondered,
why did we wait so long.
Why didn't we give him the gift,
the gift of who he was to us
long ago.

It seems very often we find ourselves
kneeling by a grave of some kind
after it is too late
wondering and lamenting at
why did I wait so long.

BODY OF CHRIST!

Christ as gift,
Christ as dialogue,
Christ as the freedom to
quietly in freedom and love
give the gift of who we are
to one another.

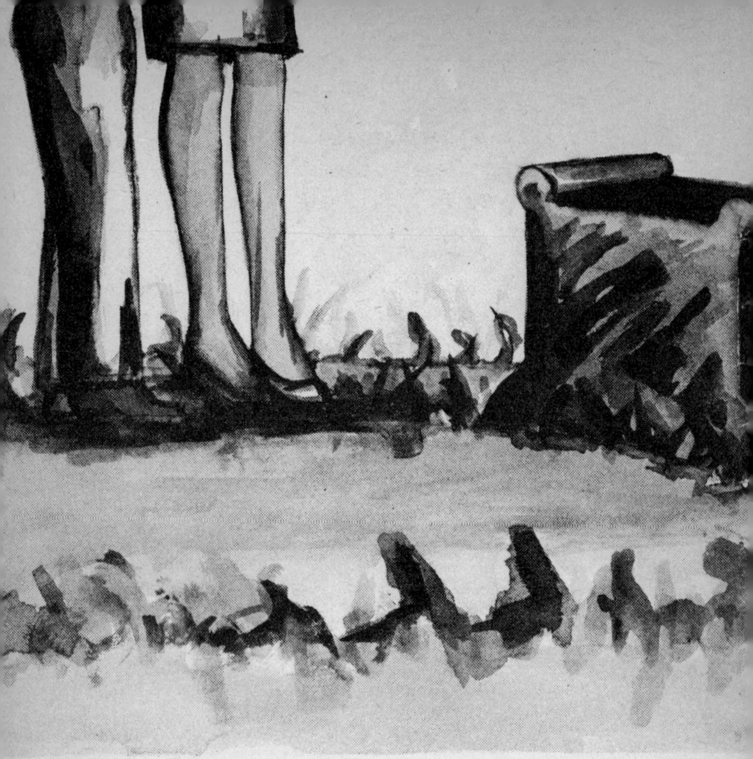

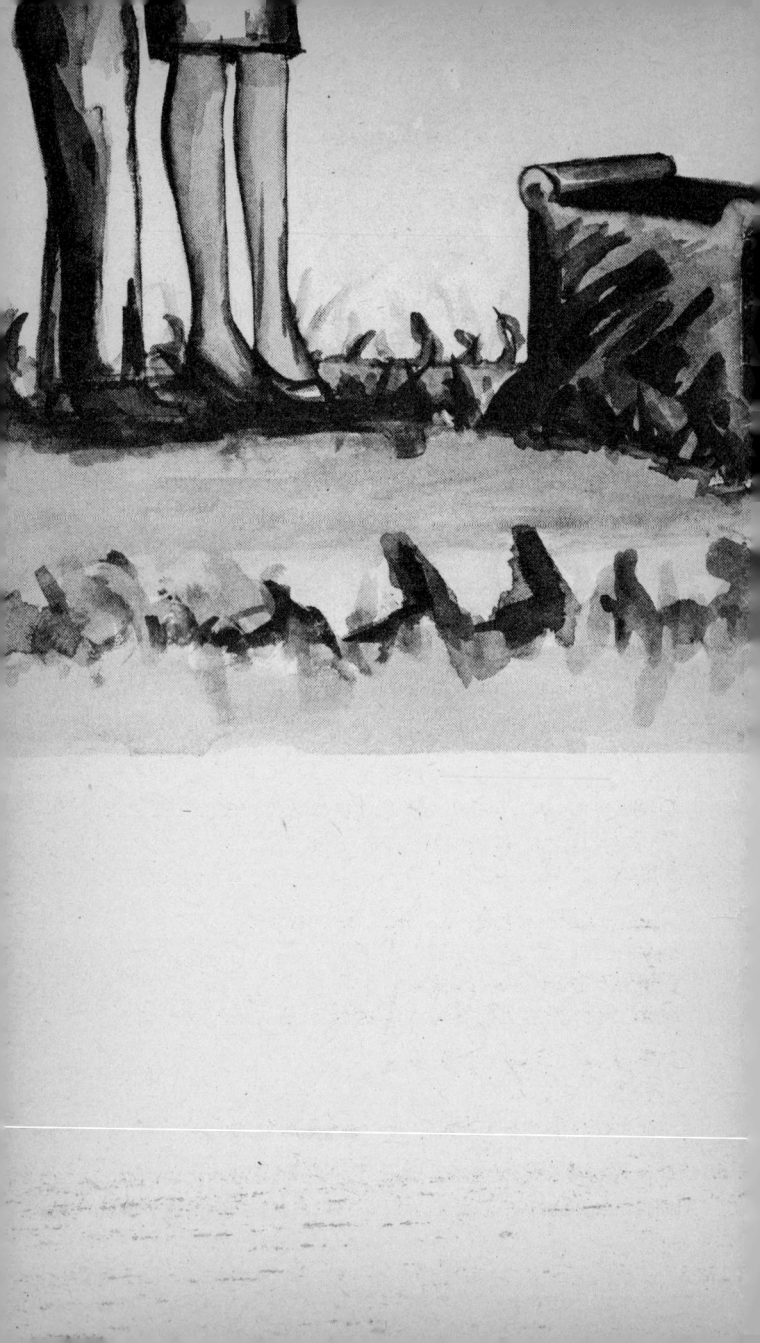

Recently I have been made aware
at the countless times I
and perhaps you
presuppose we know who we are in
one another's life.

We are so sure who we are
as the red flower of grace
to the other
that the question does not even arise.
And not being asked there is no
invitation to greater, deeper Life.

Too often we stumble around in our
unspoken richness
never thinking of speaking that word to another
and absolutely unaware that anyone
would have such a word to speak
to us.
Again,
the question of faith.

Periodically at the close of a retreat
there will be an event called a
Christ seal.

The point simply is that we often
say
Christ is in everyone,
that we are all Sacraments.

What we don't know is
HOW
we have been Christ to one another.

We don't know how the Lord has used us to
stem a fearful flight or bolster a sagging wall.

The Christ seal is run in groups.
The retreatants gather in the same small groups
they have met in during the retreat.
All it amounts to is the simple sharing
with one another,
all taking their turns
the way each has brought Christ to
the weekend.
It is usually an extremely beautiful event.

In every group there are the
Ryans and Brads,
the Johns and Eds.
There are the Jans and Caseys and
Beccys.
Few could possibly believe that
THEY
were a sign of Christ to anyone else.
But how can you dispute what they are
telling you.

Jan is told,
"I'm not sure just what it is
but
there is a wisdom and depth in you.
I look into your eyes and
somehow feel the suffering of a loving God."
Ed
hears that there is
strength in him
but not the strength he thinks.
He hears people tell him that it is the
strength of wanting to —
of not having but seeking.

He never thought of this before.
What could it mean?

Brad, the sinner, is confronted
with his humility.
Imagine his astonishment when he hears
that *he* has been the servant of the Lord
bringing comfort and light into
someone else's life.

Together we walk to the
open door.
Alone we can avoid it forever.
In dialogue we cannot.
There can be no arguing —
If I tell you this is what you brought
TO ME
who are you to argue about it.
You aren't me.
You don't know what you bring to me.
And that is just the point.
We don't know.
We can't know
outside of dialogue.
And all too often we don't tell
one another.
And so
like buried treasure
we walk around with our load of gold,
never sharing it.

For how many people are you
gold in their pan?
None?
Three, five, ten?

But how do you know?

In a sense we become
thieves
when perhaps we don't have to be.
We know those who are
precious gifts in our lives.
Those who bring humility or
innocence or humor
but how seldom we tell them.
How seldom we have the freedom to share
the real gift.
We remain thieves
sneaking their treasure through their
clear glass windows.

They might say,
"You can't steal what is given"
but they don't know what is given.
That is the point —
they,
we,
don't know what is given if we don't
share it in true dia-logue.

It is not good enough to know
in general
that we are Christ-Sacrament.
Not if we are to find and pass through
the open door.
We must also know
in particular.

We are tempted to often think
it is not important.

It leads to pride or
weakness.
I don't want to be this
big thing in your life.
I don't need to hear you say it.

On and on.
Reasons and excuses without end.

But it is important!
Important for mental health and at times
mere survival.

Were Jan given this precious gift,
this necessary gift,
repeatedly,
as we all need it
over the span of her
pain-filled life
she would not have been there the day after
Christmas,
the day of gifts,
hoping for the insane courage to die.

Tell her it is not
important.

Were more to have seen Casey,
to share with him,
to prove to him that he doesn't have to
fake insanity
to be seen
perhaps his whole life would be different.
Perhaps then he would be open to hear
Jesus say,
"Hey, Casey, I really love you."

Perhaps then
that love would be of more importance than
his fear of hell

Body of Christ,

Body of Christ —

what does it mean?

On the Feast of the Holy Family
this thought was delivered in a Mass homily.
The thought that
unless we tell one another
we simply don't know
the gift we are to another.

Most people listen to homilies
and relate to them in general.
Many are not very personal,
either in that they can be personally related to
or in that the homily is directed toward them.
It's a painful thing to be on either end of a
general homily.

And so the priest dealt with it like this:
He started pointing out people in the
congregation,
right then and there,
telling them what gifts they were
to him.

It wasn't general any more.
No one was asleep.

There was the woman with the
beaming face.

She sat there with her family,
forced to listen
while the priest told her
from the pulpit
that each time he happened to say Mass there
he hoped she would be present.

She not only paid attention during Mass
but truly prayed.
There was such a glow of joy and love
in her face that it made the Eucharistic liturgy
make ever so much more sense to the priest.
She didn't know that of course.
She was sure
to the priest
she was another face in the crowd.
She was wrong.
But how would she know.

Old Mike got his name called out, too.
Mike is 85 and mostly blind.
He is slow to get around but
his spirit is as agile
as a firefly.
He says his rosary during Mass
and has his hand stuck out for the handshake
of peace
before anyone can get there
Mike doesn't know who is around him,
he just sticks his hand out for anyone
who might want to shake it.

Who is he to the priest?

How would Mike know?
Mike just thinks he is an old man
from the nursing home,
someone has to bother with to get to Church.
How would he know what a gift he is
and always has been
to the priest.
And so the priest told him —
right there in front of everyone.

Delores couldn't know either.
As a high school girl she is fighting enough
of her own battles.
Most of them having to do with self-acceptance
and self-image.

Where in the world would she get an idea
that she could be important to that priest
way up there?

Sure,
they are friends
but he has so many friends.
And after all she is so...
so what?
And there follows a long list of doubts
and boggy self-questioning
qualities.

But what she is is lovely and kind,
she is a seeker and surrounded by all the
innate beauty that girls her age have just
because they are.

How would she know that when she comes around
after Mass
as she usually does
how important that can be.
How would she know that the priest
could easily be very down, needing to be
picked up
if the word of God is to be proclaimed in the
next Mass.
She wouldn't.
She couldn't —
if it is never told.
So there it was.

Martha is sick,
yet she was up there
leading the Christmas singing.
She has a permanent sickness than can only
get worse.
She could have been a lot of places
Christmas night but
up there singing.
Between songs she needed a chair.
She also wrote a poem to share with her
congregation after the Mass.
Giving her all.

How would she know
what a gift she was.
Martha was so concerned that her songs were
all right.
"I'll change them around
if they aren't the right ones, Father."

But she was the song.
How would she know.

At one time on an outing with a group of
teenagers
Lisa had been along.
Lisa was also at that Mass.
Someone had caught a few small fish and
put them in a bucket of water,
then gone off for lunch.
Lisa had slipped out,
gone down to the lake and
put seaweed in the bucket
"it makes it nicer for the fish."
Silly, dumb —
perhaps.
But such a wonderful touch of sensitivity
and feeling.
Did she know what that had meant to the
priest?
What a gift it had been?
How it had helped
in some small but important way
even acknowledge that the open door
could exist.
If she didn't
she found out —
right there at that Mass
in front of all those people.

There were others.
But the point is it
no longer was in general.

Love is not in general.
Nor is growth.
It is in particular.

As Eucharist is an in particular gift —
as dialogue is an
in particular gift of self
we give and receive from
one another.

Each one passes through the open door
in particular.

The attention was high at that celebration.
The Body of Christ was far more than
merely white bread.

The practical conclusion was that
just as there were
many gifts at this Mass since
people didn't know the gift they were —
what about your family?

The suggestion was made
that at the next family meal
take some time.

Don't crash into the food.

Simply share with each one
the richness
you bring into one another's life.

See if you can do it.

See if there is enough trust and freedom
to share the love you have
one for another.

Give one another
the Body of Christ.

LEAVE CHRIST

In the process of this dialogue
Christ is born.

He becomes visible and from that place
of power
initiates growth.

We, with Him,
become more visible Christians
by reason of depth.
Is anything of much more importance?

What happened to Jan
after I left?

What of Casey?
Where is he now?

Does Beccy still have her
gold necklace?
Will she remember?

What of your family spread across this country,
sons and daughters,
mothers and fathers living on
different coasts.

Who is taking care of them?

Who heals them?
What of the multitude touched momentarily
by all the organizations of charity in the Churches.

The old woman living alone,
the young boy in the hospital,
the angry man in jail —
you met them,
maybe sang for them,
maybe held their hand.

But who is with them now?
Who is taking care of them now?
You aren't there to hold their hand
and maybe right now you need
your own hand held?
Who will carry on the ministry?
Body of Christ.

So often we have not even the light
to ask the right question.
It is Jesus who heals.
It is the power of God
born in dialogue for us
that brings to fulfillment.

This of course is not to say
it is meaningless if we hold the hands
of all the Jans and Caseys in the world.
It is.

It is also important that we allow our own hands
to be held.

The point is
how often we can get into a mental depression
because WE AREN'T THERE.

But
have we given birth to at least a
part of Christ in their
lives?
To the extent that we could?

Have we brought them closer to that
open door?
Closer to accepting that
God loves you — I know
because I love you.

If so, then
Jesus is still with them.

The question of faith:
Do we believe that Jesus can do something
even without me?
If so
and if we accept his unfailing love for them
and me
then we must do our part,
plant the seed — see the unseen beauty
and leave the harvest to Jesus.

More accurately
leave them to Jesus.

Even when I am not there —
He is.

It is our task to be the servants
of New Life.

Christ is New Life.
He calls new life into being.

The Body of Christ is New Life.
We are the servants of that life.
Though nebulous and changing
our part in the wondrous process of this
New Life is vital.

In his new book "Reaching Out"
Henri Nouwen speaks beautifully,
as always,
about the need for hospitality.
For that "space and place" where we know it is
okay to be.
Where we feel at home.
Where there is a time away from fear and games,
where we are accepted for who we are and not just
what we can do.
We are a vital part of that
hospitality.
The lines are not always clear
but we are in communion with Jesus to make
it available.

I will never more be able to
view the host,
the Body of Christ,
without seeing a yellow ribbon.

It happened like this:
A young son had gotten on a wrong road,
gotten in trouble and ended up in prison.
He was released just before Christmas.

There is a tremendous cultural shock
related to getting out of prison.
Strange as it may sound
there is often great fear associated with it.
The mind has been so institutionalized for
so long
how will I make it when I am free to do what
I want?
There is fear as to acceptance back
by the community.
Fear as to whether stupid questions will be asked
about
"What's it like in there?"
Fear as to if there is a "place and space"
to come back to.
How does a young man who has seen all that
prison life is
relate to those who have not?

For five minutes when he got to the
airport
he simply walked back and forth
in amazed wonder
across the pressure plate opening and shutting
the door.
Now he had control over doors opening
and closing.
Before he did not.

What do open doors mean?

When he entered his parents' house
the first thing he saw
was a huge Christmas tree.
It had but one kind of decoration —
a dozen yellow ribbons.

Body of Christ.

What does it mean?

Perhaps yellow ribbons on a big
Christmas tree
say it as well as anything.